The
Allotment
Ghost

& Other Adventures

by Stephen Bowkett

Illustrated by Jamie Egerton
Cover design by Sandi Patterson

NEP
PO Box 635
Stafford
ST16 1BF

First published 2001
© Stephen Bowkett 2001

ISBN – 185539 081 7

Stephen Bowkett asserts his moral right to be identified as
the author of this work.

Illustrations by Jamie Egerton
Cover illustration by Sandi Patterson
Edited by Anne Oppenheimer
Design by Neil Hawkins

Printed in Great Britain by
MPG Books Ltd., Bodmin, Cornwall

Acknowledgements

Thanks to Sandi Patterson and Jamie Egerton for great
visuals, to Anne Oppenheimer for such effective editing
(as usual) and to all members of the Double Dare Gang
wherever you may be.

Stephen Bowkett
July 2001

You can read more about the Double Dare Gang in:
The Frankenstein Steps and Other Adventures

This book is part of an educational package called *ALPS
StoryMaker*, which uses fiction as a resource for Accelerated
Learning.

For further details go to www.sbowkett.freeserve.co.uk or
contact Network Educational Press on 01785 225515 or via
www.networkpress.co.uk

The Double Dare Gang

Code of Honour

- LIVE TO DARE - DARE TO LIVE!
- HONOUR THE DOUBLE DARE GANG!
- HONOUR YOUR FELLOW DOUBLE-DARERS.
- SHOW RESPECT - HURT NO-ONE.
- THE WORLD IS THE QUESTION - YOUR LIFE IS THE ANSWER.
- THE GREAT ADVENTURE HAS BEGUN.

We are defined by our choices

DDG Forever!!

Contents

Bravery Test

One of the best places to go and play was up the lane. From where I lived, you crossed the main street into Auriga road and then, instead of going over Bowden Park towards the school, you turned right. This brought you on to a long stretch of smooth path – what the town council called a 'linear walkway', but which used to be the old Kenniston-to-Clayton railway line. Sometimes the pathway ran along the top of a raised bank; sometimes it dipped down so you were in a little valley surrounded by bramble and dog-rose bushes and rowan trees. The walkway went on for miles, and in the summer was always busy with cyclists and people out for a stroll, and kids playing.

On this particular day, I'd phoned my mate Pete Clements after coming home from school. I hadn't seen Pete all day, and over the phone he told me he had a bad dose of cough and cold, and wouldn't be fit till the weekend. He made his voice sound croaky, and coughed every few seconds, just to prove how bad he was. The fact that we were having a spelling test in Mr Dilks' class tomorrow had nothing to do with it, of course.

"Well I'll come round on Saturday then, I suppose..."

"Yeah (cough cough) OK, Steve. Thanks for (cough) ringing (cough)."

"I'll tell Mr Dilks you won't be in this week – "

"(cough) You're a real pal (cough cough cough cough)!"

"See you, Pete."

2

"See you (cough) Steve (cough). Bye (cough)."

I was disappointed not to be seeing him that afternoon. I had other friends, but mostly they liked to stay in and play on their computers or watch videos. Pete and I preferred to be outdoors, especially in good weather. The sun had been shining all day; it was a brilliant September afternoon, and I was going to make the most of it.

"Mum," I said, strolling into the kitchen, kind of casually. "I'm going out for a while, OK – up the lane."

"I heard you on the phone... You're meeting Peter, are you?"

I gave a little sigh and explained that he wasn't well, but I'd only be up the lane so I'd be quite safe and in any case there were loads of people about and I wouldn't talk to strangers and no way would I take sweets from them! Honest, Mum – honest!

Mum thought about it and gave a little sigh of her own.

"Well, you must be back before it gets dark."

"Yes, Mum." It was four o'clock now, which meant I didn't have to be home for three hours or more.

"And don't you go getting your jeans mucky. Your other pair's in the wash."

"No, Mum."

"And that's a school shirt you're wearing – don't get that mucky either."

"Why, are my others in the wash too?"

"And don't you get lippy with me, or you won't be going out to play at all!"

"No, Mum. Sorry, Mum."

I thought I'd be able to escape without further hassle, but because I hadn't eaten tea yet, Mum made me up a pack of sandwiches. They were my favourites, cheese slices and tomato sauce. And I liked the tomato sauce spread so thickly that it oozed out the sides when you took a bite. Mum wrapped the sandwiches in greaseproof paper, then in a plastic bag.

"And you'll need something to drink."

"Orange juice, please. I'll have it in my canteen..."

Last Christmas my main present was an Action Guy Special Forces Survival Kit, which included a water canteen that you could clip onto your belt. Mum filled this up with orange juice, and I clipped it on to my belt. It felt really cool – because the juice had come straight from the fridge.

"I'll see you later then, Mum!"

"Don't you want your jacket, Stephen? It will be getting cold later."

"I'm OK, I'll be warm enough running away from all those strange people with sweets!"

Mum started to yell something after me, but the traffic on the main road drowned out her voice. Besides, I was too busy laughing.

* * *

Sometimes kids from the school turned up anyway, just on the off-chance of catching a good game of touch-tig or football, or cricket at this time of year. I thought maybe I'd bump into Wilko or Karl, but as I wandered along the walkway where it bordered the park, I began to feel I'd be out of luck today.

A couple of cyclists swished past me, heading out into the countryside. In the distance, the walkway ran past the golf course, and then through fields for miles until it ended at the main Clayton Road. I watched the cyclists dwindle to little dots of blue and purple dayglo brightness. Then I stopped walking and squinted – not because the sun was glaring into my eyes, but to listen harder for what I thought were the sounds of voices coming from not far away.

And the more I listened, the more I became convinced I could hear voices off to my left, over the bank and down in the tangled ground at the back of the park.

I scrambled up the bank, sniping like a Special Forces Action Guy out on a mission, and peered cautiously through the bushes. I'd been right. Down on the waste ground, five boys were playing some sort of neat throwing game. It looked like they'd collected some old tin cans and lined them up on the top of a low wall nearby. One kid pitched a stone and struck a can square-on. Can and stone tinkled out of sight behind the wall.

The boys whooped and cheered. The kid who'd hit the can grinned and got ready for what I supposed was his free bonus shot. I eased forward for a better view. A twig snapped under my foot.

The five boys glanced round and saw me, and a second later were charging up the bank to get me like a band of wild savages. I let out a little squeal and turned to make a break for it. But the leg of my jeans got tangled in a clump of brambles. I tugged furiously, feeling desperate and panicky, but thinking how ridiculous it was that I was still hanging on to my bag of sandwiches.

While I was pondering this, feeling maniac laughter rushing up from my chest, one of the kids took hold of me and dragged me backwards. Then all of them were there, whirling around me. One boy sat on my shins, and a couple of others pinned my arms to the ground. Someone snatched my sandwiches away...

Then it all went quiet. A face loomed above me – the face of a scruffy, ferretty-looking boy with a mischievous gleam in his eyes.

"Whatcha going to do, Nige?" one of the others whispered.

"Give him a Chinese Burn!" said his friend. I started to struggle because a Chinese Burn – where your enemy wrings your wrist like a disc cloth - really really hurts. But resistance was useless; all the kids did was to press down on me harder.

Nige – ferret-face – sniffed thoughtfully as he gazed down at me.

"Don't know yet. But first," he said to me, "I want to know what you were doing spying on the Double Dare Gang...?"

* * *

I'd heard about this gang, mainly through rumours and stories in the playground. These kids dared each other to do crazy things... But the person who thought of the dare was always double dared, so he had to do it too. If he didn't, he was called a yellow-belly chicken for weeks afterwards, and had to hang his head in shame. Nobody I actually knew very well belonged to the DD Gang, though I recognised a couple of kids from my English group in Year Seven; and one or two of the boys gathered round looked old enough to be in Year Eight. I wondered what awful things they did to earn them that reputation.

"Like I said," Nige repeated, interrupting my thoughts, "I want to know why you were spying on us."

"W-well..."

"Let's just duff him, Nige," said one boy, plump and hostile-looking and shaped like a peardrop. "I could sit on him!"

"Leave it out, Neil," Nige replied. "We don't want to turn him into a bookmark! Let's give the kid a chance to explain..."

"Well, I'd heard about you, right, and one of my friends in Year Seven, right, said that you sometimes came out this way to play that great-looking throwing game. So, right, I thought I'd see if it was true, right – and it was! And I thought it would be really fun to join in, so that's what I want to do, if you'll let me, please. Right?"

"Right," Nige said. He pointed his finger at my face. "But what you haven't heard is that the only kids who can play our games with us have already joined the Double Dare Gang. Right?"

"Right," I said brightly, "so I'd like to join then. OK?"

The other boys made funny expressions at one another, sort of secretive. And they were grinning, which made me feel uneasy. Nige's finger never wavered.

"What you don't know, buddy, is that there are only two ways of joining the Double Dare Gang... The first is if you've belonged to the Candoo Club. You heard of that?"

"Um – well..." I made a show of thinking very hard, but then had to give up in defeat. "Actually, no."

"The other way is to take a bravery test. Are you going to do our bravery test, kid?"

"Well – that is, er, my Mum said I, ah, had to be back home by, er, by..."

"He's just a yellow-belly chicken," said Neil, the peardrop-shaped boy. "Please let me sit on him!"

"Are you a yellow-belly chicken, kid?" Nige asked me, cocking his head sideways.

"Or are you worthy of being called a Double Darer?"

"Sure I am – what is this bravery test anyway?"

All of the boys got off me like lightning and one huge, square-looking kid who was even bigger than Neil hauled me upright one-handed.

"I'll show you," Nige said, beaming in a friendly way. "Follow me."

"Well, all right, since you put it like that," I replied; though since the big square boy still had hold of my shirt collar, I didn't think I had any choice.

* * *

We walked along the edge of the waste

ground towards some garages not far from the allotments: well, we marched actually, as though I was going in front of the firing squad. That's what it felt like, anyway, and suddenly I felt all squishy inside. I tried to convince myself it was because of Mr Dilks' spelling test tomorrow – that always gave me butterflies... Except this felt more like a flock of seagulls in my stomach.

"It's quite a nice afternoon," I said, my voice coming out smaller and higher than I'd intended. "For the time of year."

I was trying to be friendly, as well as trying to show these kids I wasn't scared. But it didn't seem to work. Nige just grinned as if he didn't believe me at all; Neil, the peardrop-shaped boy, sniggered, and the huge square kid (Wall Boy I called him in my mind) seemed not to have much of a clue what was going on. There were two other boys in the group. One of them was really skinny and had slightly goofy teeth and greasy black hair. The other one wore glasses with these great thick lenses, which made his eyes look as though they were popping out.

"I'm Steve," I said, giving the cheerful approach one last go. "Who are you?" I asked the kid with glasses. He stared right back and didn't answer.

"We don't give our names away to people who aren't in the gang," Nige explained.

"But you're Nige, and he's Neil!" I pointed to Peardrop.

"You don't believe they're our real names do you?" Nige wondered, shutting me up and making me feel more lost and alone than ever...

"But they are, Nige," said Neil.

Nige silenced him with a glare.

"Yeah, but we won't tell him that until after he passes the bravery test..."

We came to the garages. And stopped. The

square boy let go of me and Nige said,

"Right, this is it."

'It' was nothing more than a rutted track. Chippings had been put down once, a long time ago, but these had been pressed into the dirt by the to-ing-and-fro-ing cars that used the garages, and the boots of gardeners on their way to the allotments. At the far end of the track stood a barrier of chain-link fence overgrown with bindweed and nettles. In the other direction was the school-end of the Park and the shortcut that led to the church. Out-thinking me, Nige, the square boy and the skinny kid stood barring my only escape; Neil and the one with professor-type glasses put their hands on their hips and just stared.

"What's going to happen?" I asked, the last word catching in my throat because the obvious answer had come to me... They're going to make me fight the huge square kid! And he's going to make such a good job of squashing me, I'll end up looking like one of my sandwiches.

"I'm not very good at fighting..."

The words came out before I could stop them, and I didn't care. I didn't care if I was called a yellow-belly chicken and everyone jeered at me in the playground. I didn't care if I couldn't play the stupid stone-throwing game. I didn't care if I never saw these kids ever again!

That thought tripped a trigger in my head and I started laughing. It happened like that now and again. Sometimes it happened when I was being told off by Mr Dilks at school, or Mrs Williams the music teacher. It was like a door opening inside and some other part of me came running out. And the more Mr Dilks shouted, the more I wanted to laugh. One time I had, and Mr Dilks had gone absolutely purple and given me a week's extra homework...

But Nige wasn't angry. He was laughing too. In fact, they all were, even big square kid and Peardrop, whose belly was wobbling with mirth.

"Fighting?" Nige came over and put his hand on my shoulder in a brotherly way. "Who said anything about fighting, Steve?" He lifted his other hand and pointed. "Look at the garages."

There were about six of them, built all in a row but with a gap between each. They were made of breezeblocks and had flat roofs that sloped slightly backwards to take the rain to a soak-away behind. Most had wooden double doors in various states of disrepair: a couple were fitted with the newer metal up-and-over doors.

"What happens is this," Nige said. "You go up on the roof of that garage there, the first one in the row. You run as fast as you can and jump across the gap onto the roof of the second garage..."

"Is that it?"

"No. Then you run along the rest of the row, jumping each gap as you reach it."

"But I might miss and fall down between the

garages... I'll get my shirt dirty – and it's a school shirt... And I might hurt myself!"

Nige made a funny expression that had a little bit of disappointment in it, and a little bit of pain. Then a smile came to his face, though his eyes had a gleam in them I didn't entirely trust.

"But I dare you, Steve. I dare you to do the bravery test and jump those garage roofs..."

All laughing had stopped now, and the boys were looking at me seriously and deeply. I thought that all of them must have taken the bravery test at some time – either this one or something just as difficult. And if they could do it, so could I.

The feeling changed inside me, into a hardness where the panic had been before.

"All right," I told Nige, "I'll do the test... But you're doing it as well. I double dare you to jump with me."

A smile appeared on Nige's face and

spread and spread until he was grinning at me happily. He shrugged.

"I wouldn't have it any other way."

The big square boy, whose name was Brian, I found out, offered to hold my sandwiches, and gave us both a bunk-up on to the roof. This one, like all of them, was made out of sheets of corrugated iron held together with rivets... Very ancient sheets of corrugated iron held together with very rusty rivets!

"It doesn't feel too safe," I announced. The roof rivets creaked and squealed and the panels bounced gently as I walked across to measure the gap.

"You won't be on it long enough for that to matter..."

If Nige said any more, I didn't hear him. I was looking down between the first two garages. The gap was about four feet, and the drop was about ten feet. At the bottom lay piles of rotting rubbish, rusty tin cans, soggy newspaper, an old wheel-less bike frame and puddles of black water slicked with oil. And the smell of dog poop was so powerful it nearly knocked me over.

I felt the roof moving softly as Nige came across and stared with me into the gloom.

"Are you going to chicken out now, Steve?" he smirked. I clenched my teeth together and shook my head.

"No way. Are we racing it?"

"If you like. I'll give you a five-second start, OK? I've done this before," he added casually. "I sort out all the bravery tests when kids want to join the gang."

"What bravery test did you do to join?" I asked him.

Nige's face changed. He glanced at his wrist and jabbed a finger at his watch. (It wasn't a real watch, but one he'd drawn on in pen. The time said half past three, which was the end of the school day.)

"Which chicken laid the first egg?... Now let's just get on with it, we haven't got all day." And he turned away and walked back to the starting point.

I took my position beside him.

"I'll start you off," Neil called up from the lane. "I'll shout GO – and that's your signal to run, Steve. Then I'll shout GO for Nige after five seconds..."

"Let me get this just right – you shout GO, and then I go? Yeah?"

He glared at me sourly because I was taking the rise. And I was taking the rise because I felt to frightened.

"Are you ready?"

"Ready," I said, although my stomach was churning and my hands were shaking like leaves.

"OK... Three – two – one – GO!"

It was a good racing start. I pushed off

strongly with my right foot and tried to ignore the way the iron roof was swaying and groaning under me as I ran. Halfway across I adjusted my pace so that I'd finish a stride at the far end, ready to jump.

As I launched into the air, I heard Neil shout 'Go' again and knew that Nige was after me. The gap flashed by below and I landed with a clang on the second roof – nearly stumbled – then found my balance and put on a spurt.

Nige landed before I was three-quarters across. One of the boys in the lane gave him a whoop of encouragement: I saw out of the corner of my eye that they were keeping pace with us as we ran.

I reached the second gap and misjudged it slightly, catching my foot on the edge of the third roof as I touched down. I felt my left ankle twist and a sharp flash of pain stabbed up through my leg.

Nige landed lightly behind me, the rhythm of his running upsetting mine as the iron

shuddered under our shoes.

I raced him across the roof, and as the gap came up we were neck and neck, even-Steven.

I glanced at him just before we jumped – and that was my big mistake.

I knew I was in trouble straight away. As Nige leaped ahead of me and hit the next roof at a gallop, I felt myself stumbling, then falling...

Falling...

Falling –

There was a terrible second of fear. The world, which had been tilting slowly, turned swiftly upside down and dropped upwards out of sight.

My arm scraped down the rough surface of the breeze-block wall and I opened my mouth to scream – But before I could, it was filled with stinking water as I hit the puddle face-first, luckily landing on a soggy bed of newspapers which broke my fall.

I lay there for a couple of minutes as wet yellow stars drifted in front of my eyes like snowflakes, and all the different pains from all the different places in my body clamoured for my attention like pesky little kids.

For a while I didn't do anything except feel sorry for myself. In the end, it was the sound of the kids shrieking hysterically in the lane that got me to my feet...

I came out from between the garages looking like a cross between Frankenstein's Monster and the Mud Menace From Outer Space. I was soaking wet, my shirt was torn, I had cuts and bruises everywhere, and my Action Guy Special Forces Survival Kit water canteen had exploded when I came down on top of it.

All of the kids except Brian were laughing at me. He was busy finishing off the last of my cheese and tomato sauce sandwiches.

Nige was rolling around on the ground having a fit of the giggles. After a minute or so, he picked himself up and came over to me wiping the tears from his eyes.

"Oh, that was amazing! Brilliant! I haven't laughed so much for ages... You missed!"

"I know," I said miserably, noticing for the first time the big lump of dog poop stuck to the back of my hand. I wiped it on my trousers, because nothing seemed to matter now... I hurt all over – but I hurt most of all inside, because I'd failed the bravery test and would never be a member of the Double Dare Gang now.

I began to sniffle. Nige came over to me as though to slap me on the shoulder again. But he changed his mind when he saw the state of my shoulder.

"Tell you what, Steve... I don't know how long your Mum will ground you for, but when you're free again, turn up here sometime and join us..."

"But – but I don't understand," I said, not knowing whether to smile or sob. "I lost the race, and I missed the jump, and I fell down between the garages, and..."

"Yeah," Nige nodded with sparkly eyes. "But even though you were scared, you still had a go. Besides, failing isn't falling down, it's staying down. You'll only have failed if you don't come back for your next dare. Oh yeah, and you have to read and obey our Code of Honour as well. OK."

"OK," I muttered. I was too shocked to say any more.

So that was it. That was how I joined the infamous Double Darers. And as a matter of fact, I might never have gone back after that day's humiliation (and after what Mum did to me when I went home), except for something the kid with professor-style glasses said to me as we were walking back up the lane...

I'd been lagging behind the others, putting off the moment when I arrived back at my front garden gate. One of them, the kid with glasses who was in my English group, broke off from the rest and walked beside me.

"Hi. I'm Kevin Howells... Don't feel bad about missing the jump. Nige did exactly the same thing when he joined the Double Dare Gang a few years ago."

"What – you mean..."

Kevin nodded. "He chickened-out as he came to the first gap; didn't know whether to jump it or not, and dropped like a stone between the garages. The leader of the gang in those days – a kid called Bruce – did the same thing Nige did for you, and let him join."

"I feel better about it now," I said, and Kevin chuckled.

"So does Nige, I'll bet. He'd been too scared to go back up on those garage roofs - until you double-dared him today."

* * *

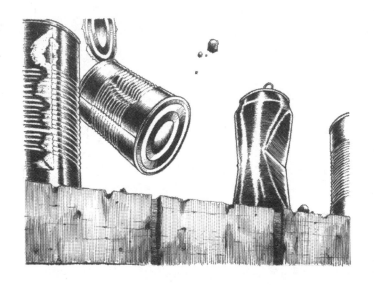

The Allotment Ghost

You could smell the apples, sweet and tempting, in the still September air. We were crouched down behind clumps of willow-herb overlooking the allotments. The purply-pink flowers had withered and died, and by Christmas the patch would be nothing more than dried sticks, giving no cover at all. But for now we were camouflaged, hidden from everyone except a small terrier who came and sniffed at us before Brian scooted him on his way.

"OK," said Nige in brisk, military style. "We go in just there, to the side of that black shed. A piece of the chain-link fencing has come loose; it'll be easy for Brian to ease it away enough for us to slip through..."

"Then what, Nige?" Neil Butler asked. He was the peardrop-shaped boy, and right now he was showing off with a pair of cheap plastic binoculars he'd had for his birthday, pretending to scan enemy territory.

Nige grinned at him. "Then we stuff as much fruit as we can into some carrier bags and get out of there!"

"That doesn't seem like much of a plan." Kevin Howells stared at us through his thick-lensed mad-professor glasses. Since I'd joined the gang I'd come to know all the regulars quite well. Apart from Neil and Kev, there was Nigel Lloyd, who was the leader of the group and a year older than the rest of us; Anthony Morris (the skinny kid) who had legs like pipe-cleaners and was the fastest runner in his school, and also the loudest burper; and Brian Roberts, a huge, square-looking boy with a huge, square-looking head. Brian was called the gentle giant by the others. He was incredibly strong, wonderfully loyal, but not very clever. Nige tended to treat him like a helpless younger brother.

"What do you mean –" Nige said, frowning at Kev, "'not much of a plan'? Have you got any better ideas?"

Kev gave a superior sniff. Behind his mad-professor glasses was a mad-professor brain. He got A's in all of his work at school, and talked about things that nobody else in the group could understand. His 'better ideas' would be worth listening to.

"Well, for a start, I think each of us should be given a separate mission. I could go to scrump apples, for example; you might go after blackberries, Nige; and maybe Steve here could collect gooseberries. That way, we avoid running around all over the place..."

Nige considered the suggestion for a moment, then nodded. "All right, good plan – "

"I also think we should let Brian stay on guard outside the allotments. If we have to run for it, we'd stand a better chance of escaping if Brian was already there, holding up the loose bit of fence for us."

"Yeah, good plan!" Brian grunted, giving a deep chuckle that set us all giggling.

"And we should make the raid when its darker – "

"I already thought of that one, Kev," Nige replied. "I reckon we should go in, say, at about half-past six this coming Friday. By then the gardeners will have gone home for their tea, and it'll be too dark for them to bother coming back afterwards."

Kev nodded in agreement, and the afternoon sun flashed gold on his lenses. "Right, I'm happier about that. The only thing I don't know yet is whose allotment we're going to raid? We can't do all of them..."

I glanced at Nige and frowned as his expression went all innocent and coy.

"Oh, didn't I mention that? We'll be raiding Old Man Jones's allotment..."

Everything went very quiet, and then Brian gave a soft little whimper.

"What's up?" I wanted to know.

Kevin was shaking his head slowly, and Neil's face had turned quite white.

"You can't be serious, Nige..."

"Why not? Just to go and scrump apples from any old allotment is so boring."

"But not Old Man Jones," Anthony whispered. "Anybody but him!"

"What's so special about Old Man Jones?" I asked cheerfully. Anthony's expression was intense. He leaned forward and glared.

"Old Man Jones is the meanest, nastiest, scariest man in the whole universe. When he's not using a shovel or a fork or a rake, he carries this big stick – And if he catches rats or mice or cats or dogs or kids on his ground, he uses it and squashes them flat!"

"He also grows the best fruit and vegetables in

town. Besides, just think what it'll do for our rep when we've pinched some of Old Man Jones's fruit – "

"No," Neil said adamantly, looking at the others for support.

"No," Kev agreed, having worked it out mathematically, I suppose.

"No," Anthony agreed. "No way, Nige."

They looked at me. But before I could answer there was a commotion not far away in the allotments. The little terrier had somehow found a way in and was scampering about among the fruit bushes and rows of vegetables...Or rather, he had been. Now he was running for his life as an enormously tall man in a black ankle-length greatcoat chased him with a big stick. Old Man Jones – for I guessed it was he – wore a battered, floppy felt hat. I could see his long white hair sticking out underneath it. And his steel-toecapped boots were enormous as he pounded along the path after the little dog. Realising that he could never catch the animal, Jones stopped, bent down and scooped up a great clod of earth, which he hurled at the terrier as it reached the chain-link fence.

The clod exploded like a bomb in a shower of soil and stones. The terrier gave a terrified yelp, dived through a gap that was too small for us to see, and shot like a bullet across the waste ground towards the garages where I'd done my bravery test, just two weeks before. He vanished out of sight and we didn't see him again.

Old Man Jones let out a roar and shook his fist in the air. Then he turned, muttering, and clumped back towards the patch of rhubarb he'd been tending.

Neil gave a squeaky little laugh.

"See, Steve, there's no way anyone in his right mind would go in there and – "

"I'm daring you," Nigel said with a slow drawl and equally slow-spreading smile.

"I'm daring all of you to raid that allotment on

Friday..."

"Well, we double-dare you then, Nige," Anthony said, opening his mouth and putting his foot in it before he realised what his words meant.

Nige's smile became a triumphant beaming grin.

"That's fine. All sorted. Now let's go and play some three-a-side football in the park – Last one there's a pie-head!"

* * *

We were, of course, sworn to secrecy. If anyone heard about our plans to raid Old Man Jones's allotment, word would have gotten round – as rumours do – with the risk that Jones himself might get wind of it. For most nights that week I was haunted by dreams of Jones in his battered old hat and his ankle-length coat hammering on our front door, coming to punish me – even though I hadn't done anything wrong yet! And in one especially scary nightmare Jones was floating outside my bedroom window, smiling a wide, white-toothed smile as he scratched at the glass with long, black fingernails...

I woke in a sweat, wondering if someone could be guilty just by thinking about a crime. I thought I'd ask Kev about that; he'd know. But there was no doubt in my mind that it *was* a crime. We were going to steal someone else's apples – on Friday – at half-past-six. And if Jones caught us, we would in fact deserve our punishment (I thought secretly, deep down in a hidden corner of my mind).

By Friday morning I was all set to pull out of the deal. I had decided to turn up that evening, at the meeting-place behind the clump of willow-herb, and tell the others I wasn't going ahead with the raid...

Then I thought about the way their faces would look, and how I'd feel, and the torment of being called a yellow-belly chicken all round the town for weeks afterwards. I'd have to leave the Double Darers and go back to doing really dull things like sitting with Pete Clements in his room playing computer games and getting beaten every time. Or moping around at home, not having anyone to play soccer with, or a good game of touch-tig...

Besides, the others had been dared too: they were probably feeling just as nervous as I was, but they were still going ahead with things... And in any case, Old Man Jones probably wouldn't even be there. He'd be dozing in his chair in front of the TV at six-thirty on Friday, wouldn't he?

Bound to be.

* * *

"You've hardly touched your tea, Stephen," Mum said that Friday. She always called me 'Stephen' when she disapproved slightly of something I'd done. "Are you feeling all right?"

"Yes, Mum. I'm just not hungry, that's all... I think I'll go out to play for a while, OK?"

"But it'll be getting dark quite soon – "

"Yeah, but if I go now I can get in a game of

football with the lads and be back in plenty of time..."

"Well, I don't know. You look a bit pale to me. Is everything all right?"

"Yes Mum," I tutted. "Don't fuss... I'm going out now, OK?"

"I could make you up some sandwiches," Mum offered. "Your favourites – cheese and tomato sauce..."

"Really, I'm not hungry – "

"What about a bottle of juice, then - you haven't drunk your milk."

"No, Mum, thanks – "

"I know you haven't got your Action Guy Special Forces Survival Kit water canteen any more, but I could put some juice in a thermos flask – "

"Mum! No! Thanks!"

"Oh, please yourself," Mum said, looking all huffed and offended. "But you're not going out in your school shirt. Remember what happened last time, you came home with it all covered in... in..."

"Doggie poop," I reminded her. "Yes, I know. OK, I'll go and change. But then I've got to go out, I really must..."

Five minutes later I went into the lounge and found Mum reading the local paper, the Kenniston Mail, which she put down on her lap as I stopped to give her a kiss.

"Enjoy your football, or whatever it is," she smiled.

"I will. I'm only down the park."

"And be home before it gets – "

"– dark. Yes Mum, I will. I'll see you sssss...."

The word sort of fizzled out in my mouth as I caught sight of something in the paper. I picked it up and read the little announcement carefully, three times, before a horrible cold feeling opened like a fist unclenching in my stomach and spread right through me.

"Oh, no... Oh, no..."

"Whatever's the matter, Steve?"

"I need to take the newspaper with me, Mum – "

"But I'm reading it, for goodness sake. Anyway, you haven't told me what's the matter – "

I didn't have time to argue or explain. As Mum reached up for the paper, I tore out the page I needed, dropped the rest, then ran for the door and belted up the road towards the park.

The sun had almost set. It was like a heap of orange coals beyond the trees. There was a coolness in the air, together with a sweet smell of wood smoke from a bonfire someone had lit in one of the back gardens along the main road.

I reached the end of Auriga Road and hurried along the walkway until the allotments came into sight. I spotted the patch of willow herb where the others would be waiting, although there was absolutely no sign of them from the path. In the allotments themselves, a couple of old guys were tidying up at the end of the day, cleaning off their tools and locking up their sheds before going home to a late tea. In a few minutes, the ground would be deserted... But that wouldn't make any difference. We still couldn't go ahead with the raid now.

I turned off the path, scrambled down the bank and hurried towards the hide-out. Nige half stood as I approached, and tried to wave me to silence.

"What d'you think you're playing at?" he hissed. "If someone spots us – "

"The raid's off," I told him, as the faces of the others appeared, all smeared with mud for extra camouflage. "We can't go and pinch apples from Old Man Jones's allotment."

"Why not?"

I handed him the page from the paper. The obituaries page.

Nige squinted in the deepening gloom to read what was written in the little black box.

43

"`Jones, Robert Charles, of Harrod Drive, Kenniston, passed away September twenty-fourth. Beloved husband of the late Martha Ann. Time passes on, but memories never fade...' "

Nige looked up at me and his eyes were big as moons. "He died. Old Man Jones went and died on us!"

"That's why we can't do the raid," I pointed out. "How could we even think of stealing apples from a dead man?"

The others, Neil, Kevin, Brian, Anthony, looked at one another, then to Nige for guidance.

Nige drew in a deep breath, held it for long moments, then let out a deep sigh.

"OK, now let's think about this... Old Man Jones lived by himself, in that big old house at the corner of Harrod Drive and Bowden Road... He didn't have any family left, as far as I know. It'll be weeks, maybe months, before the council gets round to giving his allotment to someone else. By that time, all the fruit and vegetables will have rotted into the ground. The stuff will be wasted. But if we go and take some of that fruit tonight, as we eat it we can think of Old Man Jones and honour his memory..."

Nige beamed perkily. "That's why we must carry on with the raid!"

He handed out a Sainsbury's carrier bag to each of us, instructing Neil to go and scrump some apples, Kev to find blackberries, me to find gooseberries, Anthony to go in search of plums, while Nige himself was on rhubarb patrol.

"Nothing better than raw rhubarb dipped in sugar," he slurped. "Keeps you regular."

"About every five minutes," Kev muttered.

My face screwed up just at the thought of it.

"Oh, and Steve," Anthony said. In his hand was a dripping pat of mud from the pond, which he held out to me. "We saved you some. You'll need it for camouflage."

"Thanks a lot," I said, putting it on very carefully so I didn't get a spot of it on my shirt.

We crept towards the allotments. Nige, Brian and I scurried along in a half-crouch. Neil, Anthony and Kev sniped like soldiers through the long grass and leaves. Nige led us to the spot he must have found days or weeks earlier; the place where the chain-link fencing was loose because the staples holding it to the post had rusted and come away. It straddled the border between Old Man Jones's allotment and the neighbouring one, and just about allowed space for the largest of us to wriggle through.

"But before we go in," Nige said, "let me warn you..."

He pointed to the border of loose soil that Old Man Jones had dug all around the inside of the allotment.

"Jones has scattered broken glass in there, to keep invaders out. So just watch yourselves, OK?"

Brian used his strength to pull the chain-link up as

much as possible. Nige went in, then Anthony, Kev, me, and Neil. We had some trouble with Neil; he got jammed and started to panic and squeal. Nige dropped to his knees and got hold of him by his jacket lapels.

"Neil – shut up!"

"It's hurting, Nige... There's a sharp bit digging into my side!"

"It's just a snapped staple. Hang on... Bri, pull the fence up a bit more... That's it. Come on the rest of you, help me get him through..."

We lent a hand and dragged Neil through to the Forbidden Zone.

"I got my trousers dirty," he moaned.

"Give it a rest," said Nige, as he turned to look at the vegetation spread before us.

We all fell silent, hunkered down in the shadows and the growing gloom. There was a green smell in the air. A green, sweet, incredibly tempting smell – of apples and plums, leaves, grass and rich, healthy soil. The wood smoke smell was there too like a delicate perfume. The whole world was sinking into darkness as the sky turned purple at the edges and deep, deep blue right above. One or two of the very brightest stars were out and twinkling.

"OK now..." Nige's voice was a whisper. "Give yourself five minutes. Stuff as much in the bag as you can, then we leg it out of here... But take your time. Don't panic. If somebody comes along, just freeze. No-one can see us in the shadows. OK?"

"A-OK Nige," Anthony said smartly, like a soldier. He gave a little salute. Nigel sighed patiently.

"Five minutes," Nige repeated. "Let's do it!"

We went our separate ways, and after just a few seconds I'd lost sight of the others in the gloom and was alone with my own thoughts.

What I thought about was Old Man Jones and the years of work he had put into this allotment. Although it was a mass of plants, like a jungle in miniature, there was an order here, a neatness which meant that he'd kept everything under control. All of it had been tended and cared-for and nourished. This was his place: his spirit breathed through it, and I was an intruder who had come to do damage and to desecrate.

"No, no," I muttered, easing my way past a tangle of blackberry brambles and a clump of blackcurrant bushes. "It's not like that... We haven't come to hurt your garden... We won't forget you. We respect this place, Mr Jones... Please believe me..."

Far away, a dog barked in the night; maybe the little terrier Jones had chased away. I bet it would never come back!

I walked between two tall rows of bean canes, coming at last to the stand of gooseberry bushes near the far side of the allotment. I glanced round to spot the others, but they were invisible in the night. I couldn't even hear the sound of apples being picked from the tree or rhubarb stalks being snapped off at ground level...

Most gooseberries, when you pick them, are not quite ripe: they're green and hard and crunchy and very sour, and the stiff hairs prickle inside your mouth. But as my hand ruffled about among the leaves, searching for the fruit, I felt one big goosegog that was ripe, just soft enough to give a little between my finger and thumb. I knew it would have a wonderful, fruity, mellow taste and a tangy, delicious flesh.

I'm going to eat you now, I thought. I'm going to eat you before I do anything else, so that I can honour the memory of Old Man Jones.

I plucked the gooseberry from the branch and brought it towards my mouth.

A sound broke the silence of the allotment – a tiny clinking noise behind me to my left. I glanced round, and for a moment couldn't understand what I was looking at.

There was a square outline of light in the blackness, or, to be precise, a rectangle of light, about the size and shape of a door. Then I understood that it was a door, framed by a light that had come on inside the little shed where, I supposed, Old Man Jones kept his tools.

A swarm of thoughts filled my head about how a light might have come on by itself in an empty shed in the middle of a dead man's allotment... And I settled on the rat that must have crept in there now the old man was gone, and had knocked over one of the tools, which had knocked the torch, which had rolled over and knocked the On button...

The door swung slowly open with a painful creaking of hinges, and framed in the torchlight stood the huge silhouette of a man. A very tall man wearing a long heavy coat and a battered felt hat. I could see spikes of long hair poking out beneath it...

In his hands he carried a big stick.

The gooseberry dropped from my fingers, though my mouth still stayed open, as though to receive it.

I could see the man casting about in the dimness, trying to spot where the tiny sound of the gooseberry

falling had come from. He took a step forward: one of the steel hobnails on his boots struck a stone, and a spark leaped in the night.

I was frozen, though not because of Nigel's advice. I heard the man breathing... I could hear him breathing! Although ghosts aren't supposed to breathe – and they aren't solid things – and so the big stick couldn't hurt me – it couldn't hurt me – it couldn't hurt me...

Old Man Jones chuckled softly.

"You horrible children. Get out of my allotment now... Yaaarrrggghhh!!!"

He came flying towards me with his coat hem flapping.

I shrieked, found I could move again, and bolted for freedom – faster than the terrier had done.

As I ran, I heard the others panicking all around me. Kevin Howells was calling for his Mummy. Because Anthony Morris was the fastest runner in the school, he reached the chain-link fence first, and zipped through it like a racing greyhound out of its trap. Nige got there next, then Kevin, who struggled through sobbing.

I reached the gap the same time as Neil.

"You go on," I yelled, "but hurry!"

Neil dropped to his knees and started to squirm through, caught himself on the wire and began to squeal.

"Hurry up!" I screamed. I could hear Old Man Jones pounding up behind me, maybe only ten or fifteen yards away.

Brian let go of the fence, grabbed hold of Neil by the shoulders and dragged him through, his baggy trousers pulling down to his knees. Not a pretty sight.

Now it was my turn. I started to stoop to go through – but then something exploded in the middle of my back and slammed me to the ground.

For a second, I thought Jones had hit me with his big stick and was going to beat me flat and use me as compost. But – I was still alive and still able to move. I realised what had happened. Because Jones couldn't catch me, he'd hurled a clod of soil with great accuracy, and with enough force to knock me over.

And he'd done me a favour, too, because now all I had to do was scrabble a couple of feet and I was free!

Good old loyal Brian hadn't run away; he'd waited for me, and now tried to help me as he'd helped Neil (who had vanished up the lane towards home).

"Come on, Steve!" Brian said. He snatched my arm and pulled.

I screamed as a sharp tearing pain burned like fire along my leg. I realised I'd cut myself on a piece of broken glass, but I wasn't going to worry about it now. Old Man Jones was just feet away, yelling and howling and laughing, as Brian and I ran and hobbled into the dark.

In the end, I just had to stop. Brian was built like a tank and could go on forever. But I was exhausted with pain and fear, and the relief of getting out alive.

"Thanks for helping me, Bri. You're a pal."

Brian shrugged his big square shoulders. "When I saw Old Man Jones coming towards me, I peed myself," he confessed.

I giggled and told him not to worry about it, I wouldn't say a word.

Nor, I decided, would I ever admit that I'd peed myself too.

* * *

Mum and Dad's anger at the state I was in was tempered by concern for the deep gash in my leg. When I got home, Mum marched me up to the bathroom, cleaned my wound with water, then held a cotton-wool pad soaked in TCP against the raw flesh. I did all my crying then, and was quite calm as

I told a slightly changed version of what had happened. Luckily, I was only grounded for a week.

Next day at school, I found Kevin Howells making enquiries about who had let word slip that the Double Dare Gang were going to raid Old Man Jones's allotment... Because somebody must have blabbed, and Jones must have got wind of it somehow.

Nige tried to find out too, in his year group. But we never did, and the thing remained a mystery. However, we all agreed that Jones had played a great trick on us, faking his own death and writing his own obituary, before sneaking down to hide in his tool shed until we arrived.

He had certainly taught us all a good lesson – a lesson that Nige carved out on a piece of wood and hung in our secret headquarters (Nige's Dad's garden shed):

NEVER STEAL ANOTHER MAN'S APPLES

And I could never forget that lesson in any case,
because I'd carry the scar where I'd torn open my
leg for the rest of my life.

＊　＊　＊

PS: You might think the story ends there. But it
actually ended on the following Tuesday evening. I
was in the front room watching TV. Dad was in his
favourite armchair reading the paper. Mum was in
her favourite armchair reading a magazine... So
when the doorbell rang they didn't lift an eyebrow
between them, but left it to me to see who was
visiting.

I put the hallway light on and opened the door –
and nearly weed myself again on the spot. For there
was Old Man Jones in all of his terrible glory; long
black coat, floppy old hat, huge pit-man's boots. But
instead of a great big stick, he held a Sainsbury's
carrier bag in his hand. And without a word he
handed it to me, turned and walked away into the

night.

I found out later he'd done the same thing with each of us in the DDG. But I didn't understand what his gesture had meant until I arrived back shaking into our front room, looked inside the bag – and saw that it was filled up with fruit.

The Long School Photograph

Even what happened with Old Man Jones didn't put us off ghost stories. If the weather was bad, or if we were in the mood, we'd meet at DDG Headquarters and tell each other scary tales.

Our headquarters was Nigel's Dad's shed at the bottom of the garden. The Lloyd family lived in Bowden, a village that was now only separated from Kenniston by the open space of the park. They had a huge back garden, and the shed was lost among trees and ancient giant lilac bushes. Nige's Dad had used it as his potting shed, but since he'd lost interest in gardening a couple of years ago, Nige said, he never bothered coming down here, and so the place was exclusively ours.

We'd converted the shed for our use, tacking new felt on the roof, giving the outside a coat of woodstain, and bringing cushions and stools from home. Our main luxury was the single power point by the door, which meant we could have light or heat or make coffee – but not all at once.

This particular time, a chilly, drizzly evening in early October, we'd decided to have one of our ghost story nights. Mum was happy about this, because it meant she knew where I was – safe and dry - and could phone Mrs Lloyd if I wasn't home on time. But it also meant she allowed me to stay out a bit later than if I'd been playing up the lane...

I brought milk and biscuits. Nige had boiled the kettle and was making coffee. Neil's offering was a big chocolate cake that his sister Melanie had made; Brian brought an economy bottle of cola; Anthony and Kevin both turned up with a family bag of sweets.

Nige replaced the kettle with a warm-air heater, and switched on a battery-operated lamp which cast a golden glow, comforting rather than spooky. And with the shed warming up nicely and the rich smell of coffee in our nostrils, we began to tell our tales.

Kevin told one about a picture with a shadowy figure in it that came to life. My story was about the ghost of a Welsh miner that returned home to tell his wife he'd been killed in a cave-in at the mine. Anthony told us all about being kidnapped by aliens. That wasn't a ghost story really, but it was still well scary!

We took another coffee break, then it was Nige's turn. Nige said this story was always passed on year by year to the new kids who came up from the middle schools.

He leaned over and pulled something from his coat pocket.

"What is it, Nige?" Brian wondered.

"Hold that end of it - you'll see..."

Slowly, Nige unrolled what turned out to be one of those long school photographs; the sort where the whole school is sitting in rows, looking serious and smart. At the bottom was written Kenniston Secondary Modern School, and the name of the photography company that had taken the picture.

Nige chuckled and pointed out one of the pupils.

"That's my Dad. He's the one who told me this story... And I heard it again when I first went to the school. Look at the ends of the bottom row – what do you see?"

We all strained to see something by the feeble torchlight, but the faint blur where Nige was pointing might have been a fault on the film, or the mark of old fingerprints. Nothing definite.

"What are we supposed to see?" Kevin asked, looking again without his glasses this time.

Kneinton Secondary Modern, June 1967

"Well," Nige answered, "that's what this story is about. It begins many, many years before my father actually went to Kenniston Sec - and it ended with this picture, as you'll see..."

*　*　*

I don't suppose schools have changed much in all that time. Kids were still kids, just like us, and teachers were teachers. Some of them were great fun, some of them you hated. The most hated and feared teacher at the school was Mr Evans – Jethro Evans – who taught maths.

What nobody could ever understand about Jethro was why he bothered to become a teacher in the first place. He never seemed happy, and he spent most of his time ranting and raving at the kids in his classes. Sometimes, if a class was a bit too noisy coming into the room, he yelled at them and lectured them about good behaviour for the whole lesson. They never learned anything – not even anything about good behaviour.

Being shouted at for fifty minutes was bad enough, but Jethro used to do something even worse. He'd pick on particular children, often the meek and quiet kids who hadn't really done anything wrong, and he'd try to make them cry in front of their friends. That's just about the worst thing you can do to someone – embarrass him in front of his mates. Jethro seemed to do it for pleasure, as a kind of hobby.

Most often, he'd succeed in turning some poor little boy or girl into a sobbing wreck. The other kids in the class would be pale and silent while the torture went on, not daring to say anything in case it happened to them. But there was one boy who did dare to say something: one kid who spoke up more than once when one of his friends was being tormented...

All I know about this boy is that he was quite small, with gingery hair, a cheeky smile, and loads of freckles sprinkled over his nose and cheekbones. It was the freckles that gave him his nickname – Specky. And because Specky spoke his mind and stood up for the weak and the helpless against injustice, Jethro hated him more than he hated any child at the school – especially because, no matter how much he yelled and screamed at Specky, Specky would never break down and cry. In fact, his cheeky little smile was always there; a smile that earned him plenty of detentions and many hours of standing outside the staffroom with his nose against the wall.

Specky didn't seem to mind. And although this was a war, he still kind of felt sorry for Jethro. It couldn't be very nice to be filled with such anger all of the time...

One of the things that Jethro did to make life miserable for his classes was to give each class a maths test every week. All the kids dreaded this, because if you didn't get enough marks in the test, you had to do hours of extra homework and be yelled at even more.

In view of this, some kids cheated – or tried to cheat, as best they could. Jethro used to tell his classes to revise certain formulas and equations, and these were the things they'd be tested on. To scrape more marks, some kids would write these equations on their hands, but trying to read off your hand is pretty obvious, and Jethro would usually catch those cheats and punish them hard. Other kids would write answers on their shirtsleeves, or on crib notes. They'd usually be spotted too, and roasted!

Specky used to cheat as well, of course, but because he was inventive and more determined – or maybe because he was just lucky – Jethro never caught him. Specky's cheat-notes were written on strips of paper that he pasted to the underside of his ruler or the tin of his geometry set. Legend has it that he also used invisible ink – vinegar, actually, which he could make appear by holding the note next to the radiator. Once he'd finished with the crib, he'd eat it!

Well, I don't know how much of this is true. But, like I said, Specky was inventive. Many of the cheats were discovered afterwards, when it turned out they'd got excellent marks in the test. That made Jethro suspicious, and after he'd 'interviewed' these children, by screeching at them of course, they'd break down and confess.

Specky always used to put a certain number of wrong answers into the test, quite deliberately, so that his results were good enough to avoid detention or homework, but not so wonderful that Jethro had cause to challenge him on cheating. However, Jethro had his suspicions, and on a few occasions gave Specky a grilling. Specky never admitted anything, and never burst into tears. In fact, he kept that rather cheeky little smile on his face the whole time – which enraged Jethro, as you might imagine.

About that time of year, the local photographer Mr Ben Leech (the kids called him 'Bleach') would turn up to take the school photograph – one of these great long jobs, like I've shown you.

On School Photograph Day, lesson three was cancelled. At the start of break after lesson two, kids began taking out gym benches, chairs and tables, which they arranged into rows in the little playground at the back of the school. Then, at the end of break, the whole school would assemble and be seated; the youngest kids sitting on mats on the floor, the next oldest sitting on gym benches, then kids on chairs, then on tables, and so on. Spaces would be left for staff to sit in the middle, the central space itself being reserved for the headmaster, who appeared after all the chaos was over.

Meanwhile, Bleach was setting up his camera. He didn't just hold it up, tell the kids to say cheese, and press a button. Oh, no. Because the photograph was enormous, taking it was more complicated than that. The camera was set on a tripod and aimed at one end of the rows of pupils. After the headmaster had made sure that everyone's hair was neatly combed and their ties properly straightened, he'd issue a warning that nobody should move. Because if they did, their faces would become a blur on the picture.

Then the head gave the nod to the photographer,

who pressed a button on the camera. This set a little motor running, which moved the camera slowly across the rows of faces. Inside the camera, another motor was drawing the long strip of film across the open shutter. The whole process of the camera moving from one end of the rows to the other took about three minutes.

Now, on this day, Specky's class had had one of Jethro's maths tests. Specky had cheated, and had not been caught, though Jethro was suspicious and in a foul mood.

Due to one of those wonderful and amazing coincidences that happen in life, Specky found himself sitting at one end of the first row of children, where the photograph was to start. After ten minutes of noisy bedlam, everything was ready. The headmaster made his inspection and gave his usual warning about not moving, then he nodded to the photographer.

Bleach, a tall, bald man who always seemed to be frowning with concentration, pressed the button and set the camera moving. After about a minute, when it was pointing at the middle of the rows, Specky's expression changed – his normal cheeky little smile turned into a great grin of mischief.

He'd had an idea.

And then, much to everybody's amazement, Specky scrambled up and ran round the back of the crowd. He reappeared at the other end and sat down in time to have his photograph taken for a second time!

As soon as Bleach stopped the camera, there was pandemonium. Kids were having hysterics, rolling about on the ground and falling off their chairs, helpless with laughter. Even most of the teachers thought this had been a great joke. But there was one person who did not see the funny side of it...

Jethro rose slowly from his seat and came storming over towards Specky. He was purple with fury, and intended giving this horrible little brat the beating of his life for doing such a silly, childish thing and ruining the school photograph.

Specky saw the expression on Jethro's face and realised he'd stepped over the line. He jumped up and ran to the little iron gate at the back of the playground, which led to the sports fields. Beyond the fields lies Burnmill Wood. And beyond that is the park with its big, round boating lake. The park, as you know, is still there today, though the lake is fenced off now and private. Some people say that lake is bottomless, but I don't know one way or the other. How could people ever measure that anyway?

Specky's plan was to hide in the woods until Jethro had cooled down (if he ever did, which was debatable). Since Specky was a pretty good runner, Jethro sent two of the biggest prefects in the school to catch Specky and bring him back – and not to be too gentle about it.

Those prefects chased Specky right across the sports fields into Burnmill Wood, and through the woods to the park. They dashed through the park to the boating lake... And there they found a rowing boat, overturned, a few yards out; and a single oar floating beside it.

There was no sign of Specky, nor was he ever seen again. The paper reported that he'd fallen into the water, panicked and drowned – and was lost in the bottomless black depths of the pond...

* * *

The years went by. Forty years went by. Jethro stayed at Kenniston School, never bothering to move on and get promotion. All he seemed to be interested in was making children's lives miserable, and no-one knew why. He became an angry and bitter old man.

Forty years went by, and by the time my Dad first went there, Jethro was all set to retire. It was his last term at the school, actually, much to everyone's relief.

The time came round once again for the photographer to arrive – this was Ben Leech Junior. And the kids called him Son of Bleach. In fact,

Leech's the Photographers is still going, down in the town: the grandson runs the business now.

At the start of morning break, after lesson two, instead of going to the staffroom where he used to sit alone reading his newspaper, Jethro went to the library. He didn't know why: it was as though something drew him there. In one little-visited corner was the archive room. Jethro went inside, feeling a bit dizzy and strange, and found the long box where all the old school photographs were kept. He flipped open the lid and searched for himself in last year's picture. It didn't take long. There he was with that familiar angry scowl on his face.

For some reason that may never be known, Jethro started flicking through the photographs, moving back and back into the past, watching himself growing younger and younger... But his scowling, scornful expression never changed in all those years.

Eventually, Jethro came to the picture where Specky's face beamed out at him from each end of the bottom row of children. Jethro was a young man at the start of his career, but even then that expression of rage had twisted and darkened his features.

You might think that after so long, Jethro would have smiled and admitted that Specky had played a good joke on everyone that day. But he didn't. Instead, he felt a black surge of emotion sweep right through him. For a few moments he thought it was a hatred of Specky and all he stood for... But then he realised it wasn't. It was envy. At last Jethro realised that he had always envied little Specky, because the boy was so alive, and so enjoyed every moment of his life; whereas Jethro's boyhood had been lonely and cold.

As he understood this, the bell rang for the end of break time. With a snarl of anger at confronting his deepest secret, Jethro slammed the lid back on the box of photographs, and barged out into the corridor.

Everyone was trying to get to the little playground at the back of the school: the corridors were jammed. Jethro pushed and bullied his way through the crowds, and upon hearing his voice, children cowered away or struggled to move aside as Jethro waded past.

Jethro had not gone more than ten yards, when among all the faces before him, he saw one face that froze the blood in his veins... The face of a cheeky-looking red-haired boy, with freckles sprinkled over his cheekbones and nose.

Jethro's heart gave a great thump, and he yelled loudly – STOP!

Everyone stopped, except for the little boy, who darted down a side corridor that led out on to the back playground.

Desperate now to catch the boy, Jethro began dragging and pushing kids out of the way. He was almost in a frenzy, almost crazy... Because he had to know. He had to know if Specky had come back to haunt him after all these long years.

Jethro ran along the side corridor, reaching the

playground just in time to see the boy hurry through the little gateway on the opposite side.

He chased the figure – which seemed to glide effortlessly along the ground – across the sports field to the woods, and through the woods to the park, and across the park to the circular boating lake, which some people said was bottomless.

Jethro was not a young man, and not especially fit. By the time he reached the edge of the lake, his heart was hammering and he was struggling for breath. His skin was very pale and had an unhealthy, waxy shine. He was sweating considerably.

Because he felt weak and faint, Jethro bent over and propped his hands on his knees. A frightening sensation, like a very cold stone, had settled in his chest. It was spreading rapidly through his body...

But Jethro hardly noticed. He was gazing down into the still waters of the lake, watching his own reflection. It seemed that his knotted scowl was changing, turning into what looked like an almost cheeky grin.

Then he understood that he was not looking at his own face, but at another; one that was rising up from the depths. A bloated, water-rotted face that lifted quickly towards the surface.

A small hand broke from the waters and reached out and touched Jethro's heart.

And then the darkness overwhelmed him.

* * *

Back at the school, the preparations for the photograph had been completed. Everyone was sitting up smartly, and the headmaster had just made his inspection and issued his warning for nobody to move. One of the teachers mentioned that Mr Evans, Jethro, was missing – and the headmaster was just about to ask if anyone had seen him, when the little iron gate creaked open and Jethro appeared.

All heads turned, and right away people noticed

that something was different about him. For a start, Jethro's suit seemed to be crumpled and damp. But there was something else, a change that took a few more moments to become clear...

The awful dark scowl on Jethro's face had faded. Instead, his lips were stretched into a half-smile, and there was a mischievous little twinkle in his eye.

He walked over to the headmaster, who expected Jethro to apologise for his lateness. But instead Jethro made a special request. Because this was his last term at Kenniston School after forty years, and the last chance he'd have to be in the school photograph, Jethro wondered if, instead of sitting with the staff this time, he might be allowed to sit among the children...

The headmaster wondered if Jethro had been drinking on duty, since only that, surely, could account for his strange behaviour. But Jethro did have a point, and the head granted his request.

Jethro grinned and hurried to sit down on the mat

at one end of the bottom row, next to some poor little kid who nearly pooped himself with fear.

The headmaster took his place and nodded to the Son of Bleach, who pressed the button on the camera.

The camera started to move. When it had panned halfway across the crowd, Jethro's smile broadened even further. He'd had an idea. And much to everybody's amazement, he scrambled up, ran around the back of the rows, and sat down at the other end of the bottom row, next to another poor little kid who almost pooped himself with fear.

Of course, no-one dared to move. But as soon as the camera stopped, pandemonium broke loose.

Kids fell off their chairs and rolled around having hysterics. Even most of the teachers thought this was a wonderful joke. But the headmaster, who was a very serious type, was not amused. How dare this man do such a silly childish thing and ruin our wonderful school photograph! He was purple with fury, and came storming over to Jethro to tell him off in front of everyone.

Jethro saw the headmaster's expression and knew he'd stepped over the line. He jumped up and legged it for the gate at the back of the playground. The headmaster chose two of the biggest prefects in the school and told them to bring Mr Evans back, and promptly.

Those prefects chased Jethro across the sports fields, astonished that an old man could move so quickly – as though he was gliding effortlessly along. They followed him through Burnmill Woods and across the park to the boating lake...

And there they found Jethro, floating face-down in the water. From the look of him, it seemed he had died some time ago...

The story that appeared in the Kenniston Mail suggested that Jethro had been drinking, because it was his last week at work. That would account for his odd behaviour. The story went on to say that the chase through the woods had brought on some kind of heart attack. Jethro had fallen into the lake, and either died of his heart attack, or by drowning.

That was the official view. But what never made the newspaper was that, when the photograph was developed, Jethro's image did not appear on it at all.

* * *

"All you've got," Nige said, "are these two little smudges, one at either end."

"Hold the light up higher, Neil," Kevin said. We gathered round the photograph, studying the smudges very closely.

"I reckon it's Jethro," Anthony pronounced.

"Naaa," said Brian. "It's Specky. Look, you can almost see his cheeky smile – just there."

"What do you think, Nige?" I wondered.

Nigel shrugged. "Who knows? All I hope is that

Jethro, on the last day of his life, learned the difference between being childish, and being childlike..."

And who were we to disagree with that?

Anna and the Rope Swing

"I did the Last Clap in Year Eight assembly yesterday," Neil announced proudly as we sat finishing our sandwiches. We'd been up the lane playing our favourite game of tin-can targets, before wandering over towards the Lime Pools. It was a lovely sunny Saturday morning, probably one of the last before the bad winter weather set in.

"Oh yeah," said Nige, as though he didn't believe it. "And have you got any witnesses that you did the Last Clap?"

Neil frowned. "Well no. That's the whole point, isn't it – nobody's supposed to see me do it!"

"If you've got no witnesses... "Nige began, shrugging. Then we all laughed at the hurt expression on Neil's face, which slowly turned into understanding that he was being teased. He grinned a little bit sheepishly and pretended he'd known it was a joke all along.

The Last Clap was something we double-dared each other to do now and then. You know how it goes: you've just sat through another boring assembly, and somebody or other has come in to give or talk. Nobody's enjoyed it very much, and at the end the head, all smiles, thanks the visitor for speaking on such a fascinating subject.

"And I know you enjoyed it too, boys and girls, just as much as I and the staff did. So now let's show our appreciation in the usual way..."

Everybody claps. We do little claps, where you clap just with two fingers; or crazy claps where your hands miss each other; or back-of-hand claps; or neighbour claps where you and the kid next to you slap each other's hand. Anyway, finally the clapping fades away... There's a moment of silence...And then someone does the Last Clap.

There's no doubt about it: it wasn't an accident. Somebody is mucking about.

The trick is to do the clap loudly enough so that everyone hears it, but not be so obvious that you get caught. It's hard, because most of the teachers are on the lookout for any last clappers. Grownups get embarrassed about such things.

"Nice one, Neil," Kev said, chuckling. "Did you get away with it?"

Neil's expression of pride vanished.

"No, I got caught."

"And?" I wondered.

"Grounded for a week's breaktimes, and I had to apologise to Mr Gough, who came in to talk about birdwatching."

"Tough break," Nige said. But he was still grinning. We all knew that being caught is the price you have to pay sometimes for being in the Double Dare Gang....

Nobody else was at the Lime Pools when we arrived. We had the place to ourselves, and it looked like a prehistoric paradise.

The Lime Pools had once been a quarry. But the site closed down years ago, before I was born. And the place was left to itself. I don't know if the council had arranged to have the quarry filled up with water, or whether it had just happened. Anyway, now the Lime Pools was a string of gorgeous green mini-lakes, where people swam and ate picnics, and where kids came to play. In the summer the place was always busy: I suppose it was a bit late in the year now for many visitors.

A few years ago, the council had run a path from the old railway line to the lime pool nearest the town.

And they'd tidied the place up a bit; cut down a load of the undergrowth, planted a few neat saplings, and put in half a dozen of those wooden picnic-style tables with the seats attached. There was even a patch of flat, gravelled ground where people could park their cars.

We walked by this area – which somehow looked a bit lonely with nobody there enjoying themselves – and moved on to the wilder part of the pools...

Here the land was untouched. The spiky grass grew to head-height, and on the near side of the pool were swathes of bracken, a kind of fern forest where you could lose yourself in seconds. Before I joined the Double Dare Gang, when I was younger, I used to come up here with Pete and John and we'd play Dinosaurs and Cavemen. We'd be cavemen out looking for food, and suddenly a huge T. rex would burst out from among the trees and come crashing towards us... Or a plesiosaur would rise up from the green waters of Main Pool, which was the biggest, and some said the deepest of them all... Then we'd dive into the ferns and hide, giggling and terrified, until the dinosaur lumbered away to look for someone else to eat.

That was really good fun. But I was more grown-up now, and I didn't think Nige and Bri and the rest would be interested in being cavemen.

"Now that," said Nigel suddenly, "is one dare that I wouldn't like to do..."

We'd come out through a clump of slim silver birch trees, to a place that overlooked Main Pool. The bank on this side was much lower than the one opposite. Right at the highest point of the far shore grew a huge oak tree. A stout branch jutted out over the water; and from that branch hung the Rope Swing.

Somebody, sometime, had climbed that tree and fixed the rope securely in place. They'd jammed half a broomstick through the rope at the bottom to make hand grips, and created what was probably the best but scariest tree swing in the world!

I didn't know, because I'd never ridden on the Rope Swing. Like Nige, I got cold feet and a funny wobbly feeling in my stomach whenever I thought about it.

The end of the swing dangled maybe twenty feet above the water, and was so far out from the edge that you needed a partner to help you... A small side-rope was attached to the Rope Swing at one end; the other end was wound around a root. If you wanted to go on the swing, you had to stand on the edge of the drop, and get your partner to pull the main rope close enough in for you to grab. And then, when you'd finished your swing, your friend helped you out again – he had to pull you in close enough for you to get your feet on firm ground. Otherwise, you'd just be left hanging there forever... Or until your arms got tired and you dropped into Main Pool.

Where that plesiosaur was waiting.

"Uh-uh," Kev said. "Neither would I, Nige. I don't think there's anything that would persuade me to do the Rope Swing. Even the big kids are scared of it!"

We gazed fearfully across the water; all hoping, I think, that nobody would start a stupid game of daring... Because then we'd have to start double daring, which meant we'd end up going on the Rope Swing when we really – really – didn't want to...

"Let's have a game of touch-tig!" Neil said brightly. Being peardrop-shaped, I guess he would find it even harder than the rest of us to keep a grip on the swing. His idea cheered us up, because it changed the subject.

"Great idea," Kev agreed. "What about it, Nige?"

Nige nodded, also relieved. "Yep. OK. Then we'll go down the KFC for a Zinger. Who'll be it?"

"Not me," Kevin yelped, already gearing himself up to run.

"How about Bri?" Neil suggested.

"Yes, Bri – Bri!" we all called.

Brian frowned, not too clear about what was going on.

"Aggghhh!" Anthony roared excitedly. "He's coming to get us!"

We scattered. I dived with Anthony into the ferns and we crouched there, shivering, as it finally dawned on Brian what was happening. He set off at a lumbering trot after Neil, who was the second-slowest runner in the gang, after Bri himself.

"He's like a big dinosaur looking for his dinner!" I whispered. "Like a T. Rex out hunting..."

We watched Brian disappear behind some bushes. The land became quiet and still.

Anthony gulped nervously and said, "I just hope there aren't any velociraptors around here today..."

* * *

The trouble with Bri is that he's so useless at playing touch-tig that you could hide all day and not be found.

After twenty minutes, Anthony and I scrambled

out of the ferns and started walking back down the lane. Kevin, who'd been hiding somewhere nearby, had the same idea. The three of us carried on together until we came to a curve in the path, where we heard some angry voices up ahead.

"What's going on?" I wondered, hoping we weren't going to have trouble with any big kids – or, worse still, with our arch-enemy Stonehead Henderson.

"Sounds like an argument," Kevin said. "There's Nige and – it sounds like – but it can't be..."

"It is," I said, as we rounded the corner. "It's a girl!"

"Yeeuch!" Anthony made a sign like he was warding off vampires. "It is a girl!"

Nige noticed us making all this fuss, and grew bright red. The girl turned and looked at us coolly.

"Hey – " Kevin giggled. "Nige is doing a tomato!"

"I know who she is," Anthony said as we walked closer. "That's Anna Williams... The word is she fancies

Nigel rotten."

"But what's she doing here?" I wanted to know. "Doesn't she realise she's spoiling our fun?"

Neil appeared. He was flushed and sweating.

"Where's Bri? Did he tig any of you... Hey – it's – it's – "

"It's Anna Williams," Kev said helpfully. "And she's got the hots for Nige. Right, Nige?"

"Push off," Nige snapped back, turning redder than ever. We went over, laughing, and pretended to warm our hands around his face.

"Got some bread anyone?" Kev wondered. "We could do toast!"

"What's she doing here?" Neil asked. "Tell her to go away."

At that, I saw an angry glitter come into Anna Williams's eyes. She obviously didn't like us talking as though she wasn't there.

"I've come to join the Double Dare Gang," she

proclaimed defiantly. "And you can't stop me!"

"But you can't join." Anthony sounded gobsmacked.

Anna challenged him with a glare. "Why not?"

"Well – because – well..." He did a tomato too, then shrugged and shut up.

For a start, we'd recently moved to our new secret headquarters. This was Nige's Dad's tool shed, at the bottom of the Lloyds' long back garden. If Anna joined the gang, she'd want to tidy it up, and make little curtains and do flower arrangements to put in the window... And we had also started having weekly farting competitions, which would have to stop if we had a girl in the gang...

"Well? Well?" Anna said, taking a step closer to poor old Anthony each time. He looked completely lost, and glanced desperately round at the rest of us for help.

"I know the rules," Anna told him, jabbing Anthony in the chest with her finger. "Anyone can join the gang if they pass a bravery test, right?"

She flicked her eyes towards Nige. Taken by surprise, he nodded stupidly.

"Um, well, yeah. But – "

"But what?"

Anna sounded really cross, like Mr Hughes the headmaster after someone's done the Last Clap.

"But, I mean, like, well, it's a bravery test. And, well – "

"Well?"

"You're a girl."

Anna turned white with fury. I thought for a second she was going to throw her best punch right at Nigel's nose. Instead, she pushed her dark hair away from her eyes and squared up to him.

She's quite a pretty girl, I thought. And she has plenty of guts. Maybe she wouldn't be such a disaster...

"Listen, Lloyd, you give me any bravery test you like, and I'll do it."

Nige sniffed and chuckled. "Yeah, well it's all right for you to say that – "

"I mean it. Any test you like... I dare you..."

A hush descended as those vital words were spoken. It was a standoff. Now Nige would be forced to let Anna take a bravery test. And if she passed...

I thought Nige would say she had to race him across the garage roofs, as I did. But he was cleverer than that. I saw him glance to his left, towards the Main Pool.

"OK Anna, if that's how you want it." He glanced at his drawn-on watch. "It's just half-past ten now. By eleven o'clock, you must have ridden on the rope swing – "

I heard Anthony give a little gasp of fear, for her sake. And I thought to myself – before I could stop it – that Nige just wasn't being fair. No-one could ride the rope swing alone; it was dangerous; it was stupid.

"Nige – " I started to say, but he hadn't finished.

"Oh yes, and that's not all. Before you go on the swing you've got to touch-tig each of us – because you're it!"

At the magic words, as though a button had been pushed, we started to scatter.

I saw Bri wander out from behind the bushes, looking bewildered.

"What's happening?" he asked.

Anna went up to him and whacked him hard in the chest.

Then she started off after Neil, who was labouring along the path, puffing like a steam train.

Anna caught up with him easily. She slammed him in the back with the flat of her hand. Neil toppled, his momentum sending him skidding along the gravel on his stomach.

"He looks like a beached whale!" Anthony chuckled. But then the smile was wiped from his face as Anna turned and came belting towards us.

We both shrieked and I dived for cover among the ferns.

Anthony, being the fastest kid in the school, took off at a sprint along the path. I saw to my relief that Anna was going after him instead of me...

And as far as I could tell, she seemed to be catching him up.

* * *

I waited for fifteen minutes, long after all the noises of shouting and calling had died away. There was just the faint crinkling of the ferns in the warm air, and the sound of my own breathing. No trace of Anna or the others. And the velociraptors too seemed to have wandered away by now...

Finally, when I thought I was safe, I came out of my hiding place and saw that the Lime Pools appeared to be deserted. Across Main Pool, the

Rope Swing hung unoccupied. I could either follow the path to reach it – easier but longer – or take the cross-country route through the undergrowth.

I chose this way, and battled through brambles and bracken and the odd patch of nettles, until I found myself on the higher ground of the opposite shore, with the great oak and the Rope Swing itself directly ahead.

I heard a commotion in the bushes and Nige and Anthony emerged. They did not look happy.

"She never tigged you?" I said to Anthony. He nodded glumly.

"She grabbed me by the brambles."

"Ouch. Must have made your eyes water..."

"It's not funny," Nige muttered crossly. "Did she tig you, Steve?"

"No. I've seen nothing of her... Here's Kev – and Neil – hi!"

Their faces were as long as Nige's, and I guessed

the worst.

A few minutes later, Bri came along. We all stood around not quite knowing what to do.

"OK." The firmness in Nige's voice broke the spell of stale silence.

"You and I, Steve, are the only ones that Anna has not tigged."

I looked at my watch. "She's still got ten minutes to go: plenty of time to turn up and tig us. I mean, since she caught up with Anthony..."

"Don't remind me," Anthony began.

Nige grinned broadly.

"But she won't tig us – not both of us anyway. I've got the perfect plan to stop her."

"Which is?" Kev wanted to know.

Nige laughed aloud. "I'll go on the Rope Swing!"

A couple of us started to argue. But Nige was determined.

"It's the only way. I mean, we can't have a girl in the Double Darers, can we? Girls are useless."

Kev and Neil were protesting because of the possible danger to Nige. But I was thinking how unfair it was to take Anna's chance away from her. She had agreed to the dare, and now Nige was making it impossible for her to carry it out.

I was just about to open my mouth and say something, when Nige glanced at me sharply.

"Steve, you partner me – get hold of the side rope."

I could have made a stand. I could have told Nige what I thought of him and his stupid pathetic plan... But then I thought how awkward he could have been when I'd wanted to join the gang. He'd let me in even though I missed the jump and fallen down between the garages. He'd done me a favour, and I owed him one back...

So I meekly went over to the oak tree and unwound the side rope from the root.

As Nige got ready on the quarry edge, I hauled the Rope Swing closer until he could lean out and grab the broomstick hand-grips.

"OK Steve," he said excitedly, "let the slack out – NOW!"

With a great shriek and a yell, Nige launched himself out into empty space, swinging in a great arc that took him way out over the water, twenty feet above the bottle green surface.

"Woo-wee!" he cried. "This is brilliant!"

I was too busy to notice at first, taking care to flick out enough of the side rope so that Nige didn't get jerked up suddenly; but being careful also not to let go of the end. If I had, Nige would have been left dangling helplessly above Main Pool once the Rope Swing had come to a rest.

After a couple of minutes, though, as the swinging diminished, I was able to stand and watch with the others. Nige was sailing weightlessly to and fro, his scraggy hair streaming behind him, his shirt flapping in the breeze.

"Are you all right Nige?" Kev called out: Nige had gone quiet, and his eyes had closed.

"It's amazing," he said in a subdued voice, which grew louder and then quieter as he swung towards us and away. "It's like being in orbit..."

Then he said nothing more, and we fell silent with him; just watching, envying him but feeling fearful just trying to imagine what it would be like to ride the Rope Swing.

After five minutes, Kev stirred himself from his daydream.

"Well," he said with a sneer in his voice, "it doesn't look like Anna's going to show up... Mind you, I'm not surprised. I would've expected a girl to bottle out of it.

Neil nodded in vigorous agreement. "Yeah, she's a yellow-belly chicken, like they all are!"

The swing had come to rest now, and Nige was

hanging peacefully in mid-air with a smile on his face as though he'd taken a swig of his mum's best sherry.

"What's the time now?" he asked.

"Three minutes to eleven," Kev said.

"OK. I'll just hang around here until after the hour, just to make sure."

"Yeah," Neil called, still smarting over being tigged, "but she's not going to come now... She's just a yellow-belly chicken, Nige... She's just a girl..."

Then we all jolted at a loud rustling of leaves nearby. We looked back through the bushes and the bracken, searching for a sign of Anna approaching. I got ready to drop the side rope and run, so she wouldn't tig me...

But she'd been cleverer than that. She'd been cleverer than any of us.

"No..." Kev's mouth dropped open in disbelief, as the screen of golden oak leaves above the big branch parted, and Anna's face appeared. She was grinning.

"How long has she been up there?"

"Long enough to hear you call her a yellow-belly chicken, Neil," I said, smirking at him.

Anna took no notice of us: she had a mission.

Before any of us could say anything more, and before Nige could act, Anna crawled along the big branch, swung herself down, grabbed hold of the Rope Swing at the top, then shinnied down it...

She shinnied down Nige, too, and grabbed hold of the broomstick handle, so that she was facing Nigel, nose to nose.

"Give us a kiss, big boy," Anna chuckled, and Nige copped a great big wet one on the lips.

His shriek was drowned out by us laughing, so much that Bri was almost sick, and Kev winded himself and had to sit down.

"Hey Nige," Anthony called out, "you're doing another tomato!"

"Steve – Steve!" Nige sounded desperate. "Pull me in – quick! Pull me in, man. She's going to kiss me again!"

He was twisting on the rope like a fish on a line, trying to keep his face out of range.

"Have you got any sweets, Nige?" I wondered casually.

"What? No, I haven't – But never mind that, just get me down!"

"I saw you eating peppermints earlier," I reminded him.

"... Oh, all right, you can have a peppermint – "

"But I want a whole packet, Nige..."

He tried to twist round and glare at me. I tried to keep the grin off my face.

"Yes, yes, a packet. Just get me – "

"I want two packets now," I called.

"And a bubble gum for each of us," Kev chipped

in.

"And a packet of crisps – brown sauce flavour," Neil said.

"Bag of those pink marshmallow shrimps," Brian added. "They're my favourites."

I guess it was going to take Nige two weeks' pocket money to pay for all these sweets, but in the end we were satisfied.

I started to pull him in.

It was hard work, because there were two of them on the Rope Swing: Nige keeping his face screwed up and turned aside, and Anna, who was looking at me seriously. I knew what her eyes were saying – that I was the only one stopping her from joining the Double Dare Gang. I was the only one left to tig.

And I thought then that Anna had been braver and smarter than any of us. She'd been given the challenge, and had planned it all carefully, even daring to go on the Rope Swing (though it hadn't been swinging at the time). And she'd done it all because she fancied Nige.

I was almost jealous of him.

As I hauled the swing in closer, Anna let go with one hand, and held it out for me to help her on to firm ground. I saw Kev's expression of shock as he realised what was happening.

But before he could stop me, I grabbed her and pulled her clear.

"Thanks, Steve," she whispered, stepping aside so Nige could jump clear of the swing.

* * *

As it turned out, Anna became the first and only female member of the gang. And it was fine. She didn't boss us around, or try to tidy up our shed. She didn't make little curtains and flower arrangements. And she even joined in our farting competitions...

She won once, too. But Brian was off that week with the flu. He usually beat the rest of us, because he was a big square kid, with a big square head, and he did these really big square farts.

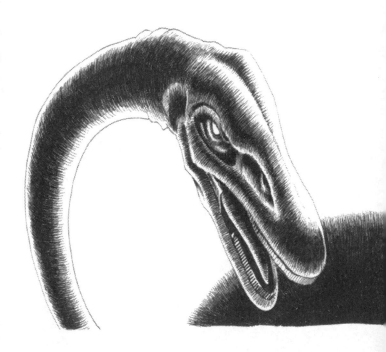

About the Author

I was born and raised in the mining valleys of South Wales. My favourite place to play was out on the hills where my imagination had plenty of space to expand.

When I was ten I joined the Double Dare Gang. We used to dare each other to do things, but the one who made up the dare was double dared, so we all had to do the dare. If you didn't you were a yellow-belly chicken. And if that happened more than three times you were thrown out of the gang!

My family moved out of Wales when I was thirteen. I went to a new school where one of my subjects was French. Because I had never learned any French, my teacher made me sit in the naughty corner and 'get on with something constructive'. That's when I started to write, just for myself, and

I've been writing ever since.

I have always loved BIG IDEAS, and so I enjoy writing fantasy and science fiction. And because I like a scary story I also write Horror. I think Horror stories are like the fairytales of old, and can teach you important things.

I am in my forties on the outside, twelve on the inside and I'm a Capricorn. I like rock music, Indian and Chinese food, and I enjoy drinking beer. I live in a small village with my wife, two llamas, two ducks, four cats, six goats, several chipmunks, ten hens, and lots of rabbits and guinea pigs.

All in all, I'm pretty happy really.

If you'd like to find out more about me and my books, go to:

www.sbowkett.freeserve.co.uk

Steve Bowkett

Other Publications

Spellbinder (teen fantasy) - Gollancz 1985 / Tellerup 1986 / Pan 1988

The Copy Cat Plan – (comic play) - Blackwell 1986

Gameplayers (teen fantasy) - Gollancz 1986 / Pan 1988

Dualists (teen fantasy) - Gollancz 1987 / Pan 1989 / Praha 1993

Catch & Other Stories (teen genre) - Gollancz 1988 / Pan 1990

Frontiersville High (teen SF) - Gollancz 1990

The Community (adult horror) - Pan 1993

The Bidden (adult horror) - Pan 1994

A Rare Breed (adult horror) - Pan 1996

Panic Station (teen horror) - Henderson 1996 / Gallimard 1996

Dinosaur Day (young fantasy) - Heinemann Banana Book 1996

For The Moon There Is The Cloud - (tales in the Zen tradition) - Collins, Pathways Reading scheme, 1996.

The World's Smallest Werewolf - Macdonald, Shivery Storybooks 1996.

Meditations For Busy People (How To Stop Worrying & Stay Calm) -

HarperCollins 1996 (USA 1996 as A Little Book Of Joy).

Dreamcastle (pre-teen SF), Orion Children's Books 1997 / Mondadori, Italy '97 (also Germany, Portugal, Norway, France and China).

Dino Discoveries (non-fiction 7+) - Henderson FunFax Dinosaur file, 1997.

Imagine That! *A Handbook Of Creative Learning Activities for the Classroom*, Network Educational Press, 1997.

Another Girl, Another Planet (adult SF, with Martin Day) - Virgin New Adventures, 1998.

Roy Kane - TV Detective - A&C Black's Graffix series, 1998, p/b '99.

Self-Intelligence - *A Handbook for Developing Confidence, Self-Esteem & Interpersonal Skills*, Network Educational Press, 1999.

Dreamcatcher - for Orion's Dreamtime teen fantasy/horror series, Spring 2000. (Steve is also Consultant Editor for this series).

Horror At Halloween / Eleanor – a Horror novella which is one segment of a 'mosaic novel', Pumpkin Books, Spring 2000.

The Planet Machine – a science fiction story for A&C Black's new Comix series, winter 2000, p/b spring 2001.

Catch & Other Stories – p/b genre stories for 10+, Crazy Horse Press, 2000.

Ice (The Wintering book 1) – Fantasy/SF saga for 11-upwards, Orion 2001.

<u>Internet@file-online.com</u> – a fun wallet for kids on using the 'Net, Top That 2001.

What's The Story? – games and activities for creative storymaking. A&C Black, 2001.